THE POWER OF CAPABILITY STATEMENTS

Craft Compelling Capability Statements for Government Contracts & Win

SMART2GO Training®

All rights reserved. No part of this book may be reproduced or transmitted in any form or by any means, electronic or mechanical, including photocopying, recording or by any information storage and retrieval system without written permission from the author, except for the inclusion of brief quotations in a review.

Disclaimer/Terms of Use

In no way is it legal to reproduce, duplicate, or transmit any part of this book in either electronic means or in printed format.

Recording of this publication is strictly prohibited and any other storage of this document is not allowed unless with written permission from the publisher. All rights reserved.

The information provided herein is stated to be truthful and consistent, in that any liability, in terms of inattention or otherwise, by any usage or abuse of any policies, processes, or directions contained within is the solitary and utter responsibility of the recipient reader. Under no circumstances will any legal responsibility or blame be held against the publisher for any reparation, damages, or monetary loss due to the information herein, either directly or indirectly.

Respective authors own all copyrights not held by the publisher. The information herein is offered for information and education purposes solely and is universal as so. The information is without contract or any type of guaranteed assurance.

Contents

Disclaimer/Terms of Use iii

Introduction 1

Analyzing Your Target Client..7

Identifying Key Differentiators 9

Crafting a Clear Value Proposition...17

Compiling Case Studies and Relative Projects............................21

Effectively Summarizing Your Core Competencies 31

Acceptable Formats for Presenting Core Competencies...........33

Resources...35

Introduction

SMART2GO Training® empowers its learners to BE. SMART. Delivering a quality learning experience by providing specialized training in real estate, leadership, personal and professional, and financial development.

A Capability Statement is a concise document or presentation that outlines a company's abilities, qualifications, and unique selling points. It is often used in marketing and business development to demonstrate to potential clients or partners reasons your company is ideal for the job.

This book will cover five (5) key elements to crafting a compelling Capability Statement. They are as follows ~

- Analyzing Your Target Client

- Identifying Key Differentiators

- Crafting a Clear Value Proposition

- Compiling Case Studies and Relative Projects

- Researching Metrics for Evaluations

You will be able to use this book as a ready-reference for any future Capability Statements you need for the multitude of government contract offerings you may encounter.

You'll notice this 💡 at the end of each segment. We encourage you to do the tasks along the way. It will make the process much easier!

Learning each step in this process will help you to understand how the client is viewing your company. If you need an attractive template for completing the tasks in this book, you can find one at smart2gotraining.com/shop. There you will find One-Page, and Two-Page options.

Thank you for allowing SMART2GO Training® to guide you in this process.

BE. SMART.

Why is a Capability Statement Important in the Government Bidding Process?

A capability statement is a crucial document in the government's bid proposal process for several reasons. It serves as a powerful tool for businesses to communicate their qualifications, expertise, and ability to meet the specific needs of government agencies. Here are some data-backed reasons why a capability statement is considered important in this context:

1. Compliance with Government Requirements

Government agencies often have stringent requirements for contractors. A well-crafted capability statement ensures that businesses can clearly demonstrate their compliance with these requirements. According to the U.S. Small Business Administration (SBA), a capability statement helps small businesses meet the criteria set forth in government solicitations, including technical expertise, past performance, and financial stability. This compliance is critical for being considered a viable candidate in the competitive bidding process.

2. Facilitates Market Research for Government Agencies

Government agencies use capability statements as a primary source of information when conducting market research. A report by the Government Accountability Office (GAO) emphasizes that agencies rely on capability statements to identify potential vendors who can fulfill their needs. These statements provide a concise overview of a company's qualifications, making it easier for procurement officers to shortlist potential contractors for further consideration.

3. Demonstrates Past Performance and Reliability

One of the key factors in government contracting is a contractor's past performance. A capability statement allows businesses to highlight previous government contracts, successful project completions, and customer satisfaction metrics. The Federal Acquisition Regulation (FAR) Part 42 highlights the importance of past performance as an evaluation criterion in government contracting. By showcasing past successes, businesses can build trust and demonstrate their reliability and capability to handle government projects effectively.

4. Enhances Competitive Advantage

In a competitive bidding environment, differentiating oneself from other contractors is vital. A survey conducted by Deltek, a leading provider of enterprise software and information solutions, found that businesses with well-developed capability statements were more likely to win government contracts compared to those without. This is because a capability statement clearly articulates a company's unique value proposition, competitive advantages, and technical expertise, making it easier for government agencies to recognize the benefits of selecting that business.

5. Streamlines the Procurement Process

A clear and concise capability statement can significantly streamline the procurement process for both the contractor and the government agency. According to the National Institute of Governmental Purchasing (NIGP), a well-structured capability statement helps procurement officers quickly assess a business's qualifications and suitability for a project. This efficiency not only saves time but also enhances the overall effectiveness of the procurement process, leading to faster decision-making and project initiation.

6. Builds Credibility and Professionalism

Presenting a polished and professional capability statement helps businesses build credibility with government agencies. According to the General Services Administration (GSA), a well-prepared capability statement reflects a company's professionalism and readiness to engage in government contracting. This professional image can be a deciding factor in winning contracts, as it assures government officials of the contractor's seriousness and commitment to delivering high-quality services.

7. Supports Networking and Relationship Building

Capability statements are not only used in the bid proposal process but also play a crucial role in networking and relationship building. The SBA suggests that businesses use their capability statements when attending industry days, matchmaking events, and other networking opportunities. Having a succinct document that outlines the company's capabilities helps facilitate meaningful conversations and establishes connections with government officials and prime contractors, potentially leading to future business opportunities.

Conclusion

In conclusion, a capability statement is a vital document in the government bid proposal process due to its ability to ensure compliance with requirements, facilitate market research, demonstrate past performance, enhance competitive advantage, streamline procurement, build credibility, and support networking efforts. By effectively communicating a business's qualifications and strengths, a capability statement increases the likelihood of securing government contracts and successfully navigating the competitive landscape of government procurement.

💡 Are there any other reasons you can list that may be relatively important to you in submitting your capability statement with your proposal?

Analyzing Your Target Client

Understanding your target client is the foundation for creating an effective capability statement. A one-size-fits-all approach is rarely successful, as different clients have unique needs, challenges, and priorities. By taking the time to analyze your target audience, you can tailor your message and demonstrate a deep understanding of their specific requirements.

The first step in analyzing your target client is to identify their industry and the type of organization they represent. Are they a government agency, a private company, a non-profit, or something else? Each sector has its own language, pain points, and decision-making processes that you need to be familiar with.

Next, research the specific organization itself. What is their mission, values, and strategic goals? What challenges or pain points are they currently facing? Understanding their motivations and objectives will help you position your capabilities as a solution to their problems.

It's also crucial to understand the decision-makers and stakeholders involved in the procurement process. Who are the key players, and what are their roles and responsibilities? What criteria will they use to evaluate potential vendors or service providers?

To gather this information, you can:

- Review the organization's website, annual reports, press releases, and other publicly available materials
- Leverage your network and industry connections to gain insider insights
- Attend industry events, conferences, or webinars where the organization participates

- Conduct informational interviews with current or former employees (if possible)

Once you have a solid understanding of your target client, you can begin to tailor your capability statement to address their specific needs and priorities. For example:

- If they are a government agency focused on cost-effectiveness, you might emphasize your ability to deliver high-quality services within strict budgetary constraints.
- If they are a private company seeking to stay ahead of the competition, you could highlight your innovative solutions and cutting-edge technologies.
- If they are a non-profit organization dedicated to a particular cause, you could align your messaging with their mission and values.

By demonstrating a deep understanding of your target client, you can create a capability statement that resonates with them and positions your company as the ideal solution to their challenges.

Write down the names of the key stakeholders in your upcoming bid? Next to their names, write down their roles and how you may leverage this information.

NAME	ROLE

Identifying Key Differentiators

In a competitive marketplace, it's essential to identify and articulate your key differentiators – the unique qualities, capabilities, or advantages that set your company apart from others in your industry. A well-crafted capability statement should highlight these differentiators, demonstrating why a potential client should choose your firm over others.

The process of identifying your key differentiators begins with a comprehensive assessment of your company's strengths, capabilities, and value proposition. Consider the following:

- Expertise and Experience:

A team with expertise is guaranteed to possess the skills and knowledge needed to complete projects quickly and successfully. Thorough training and certifications are common ways for professionals to obtain specialized knowledge and abilities, as they attest to their suitability for managing particular tasks. In contrast to a company with generalist abilities, a software development company with certified developers in many programming languages and frameworks is more likely to produce innovative and robust solutions.

When a team is proficient, they guarantee that they have the right knowledge and abilities to complete tasks quickly and successfully. A professional's capacity to perform particular tasks is confirmed by certifications and extensive training, which are common ways to obtain specialized knowledge and abilities. Software development companies with certified developers in many programming languages and frameworks, for example, are more likely to produce innovative and reliable solutions than companies with generalist abilities.

Experience enhances knowledge by offering useful perspectives and the ability to solve problems in the actual world. Years of experience in a specific field or business help people hone their abilities and create best practices. A team with experience is better at foreseeing problems and putting workable solutions in place, which improves the quality of the finished good or service. Here are some questions to consider:

1. What specialized knowledge, skills, or certifications does your team possess?
2. How many years of experience do you have in your industry or niche?
3. What types of projects or clients have you worked with?

- Service Offerings and Capabilities:

A company's service offerings are the particular goods or services it offers to satisfy the needs of its customers. They establish the value proposition and form the center of the company. Potential customers can better grasp what to anticipate from the business with the aid of a compelling and unambiguous service offering. Additionally, it matches firm activities to what the market demands.

Businesses looking to improve their online presence, for example, can find a clear value proposition from a digital marketing agency that provides services like SEO, content marketing, and social media management. By specifying these services precisely, the agency may draw in the correct customers and establish a solid reputation in its field.

A company's special techniques, procedures, or equipment for providing its services are all included in its capabilities. In a saturated market, these features frequently function as differentiators. A business that possesses exclusive techniques or cutting-edge equipment can provide a special offering that rivals might not.

Questions to consider:

1. What specific services or products do you offer?
2. Do you have unique methodologies, processes, or tools that set you apart?
3. Can you provide end-to-end solutions or are you specialized in certain areas?

- Resources and Infrastructure:

The term "resources" refers to the material and immaterial assets—such as trained workers, cash, equipment, and technology—that a business can utilize. The organizational and physical frameworks required for the operation, including as office buildings, manufacturing facilities, IT systems, and management frameworks, are referred to as infrastructure. When combined, they show how operationally capable a business is.

Highlighting Competitive Advantage

In a competitive market, infrastructure and resources can make a big difference. Businesses that make investments in cutting-edge technology, reliable systems, and knowledgeable staff are better able to provide services than those that have fewer resources. An organization can draw attention to its competitive advantage by highlighting these resources in a capabilities statement.

For example, a tech business can set itself apart from competitors with state-of-the-art research facilities, a group of very talented developers, and unique software tools. This demonstrates to prospective customers that the business can not only meet their immediate demands but also innovate and grow to meet new difficulties.

Demonstrating Readiness for Large and Complex Projects

A corporation demonstrates its capacity to manage a range of projects when it offers information about its infrastructure and resources in a capability statement. For instance, a construction company can reassure prospective clients of its capacity to handle major building projects successfully and efficiently by showcasing its fleet of equipment, cutting-edge tools, and staff of trained engineers.

1. What physical resources, facilities, or equipment do you have access to?
2. Do you have proprietary software, databases, or other technological advantages?
3. How large is your team, and what is the breadth of their collective expertise?

• Approach and Philosophy:

Decision-making inside the organization is framed by a philosophy and strategy that are well-articulated. A unified and consistent delivery of services is ensured by this framework, which makes sure that all personnel share the company's beliefs and ideals. An ethical consulting firm, for instance, would advise its staff to follow these standards in all projects and to make decisions based on confidentiality regarding clients. The organization's integrity and internal culture are strengthened by this consistency, which also helps the clients.

Understanding and agreeing with the company's strategy and attitude increases the likelihood that a client will be involved and satisfied. Collaboration and partnership are fostered by this knowledge. In the event that a customer and environmental consulting firm have similar environmental principles, the client will be more involved in the project and feel more dedicated to sustainability. Client satisfaction may increase as a result of this alignment and more successful results.

Some important questions to ask are:

1. What is your company's mission, values, and guiding principles?
2. How do you approach client relationships and project management?
3. Do you have a unique perspective or approach that sets you apart?

Once you have a clear understanding of your strengths and capabilities, you can begin to identify the factors that truly differentiate you from your competitors.

Consider:

- What do you excel at compared to others in your industry?
- What unique value or benefits do you provide to clients?
- Are there any niche areas or specialized expertise that you possess?
- Do you have proprietary processes, technologies, or methodologies?
- Can you offer faster turnaround times, better pricing, or superior customer service?

It's important to be specific and quantifiable when identifying your differentiators. Instead of simply stating that you have "experienced staff" or "high-quality services," provide concrete examples or metrics that demonstrate your expertise and excellence.

For example:

- ➤ *"Our team includes five Certified Project Management Professionals (PMPs) with an average of 10+ years of experience in complex Communications implementations."*
- ➤ *"Our proprietary software development methodology has been proven to reduce project timelines by 25% while maintaining strict quality standards."*
- ➤ *"Our state-of-the-art manufacturing facility is ISO 9001:2015 certified, ensuring consistent quality and adherence to industry best practices."*

By clearly articulating your key differentiators, you can create a compelling capability statement that highlights the unique value and advantages that your company can offer to potential clients.

The capability statement is more professionally written when it includes specific and measurable differentiators. Thoroughness and attention to detail are reflected in a well-written statement that contains particular data points and examples. It implies that the business is dedicated to openness and responsibility in addition to having faith in its own talents. Gaining the favor of possible customers may depend heavily on your professionalism.

List as many of your key differentiators are you can below. Add a sheet, if necessary.

Crafting a Clear Value Proposition

At the heart of an effective capability statement is a clear and compelling value proposition — a concise statement that communicates the unique benefits and value that your company can provide to potential clients. A well-crafted value proposition serves as the foundation for your entire capability statement, succinctly encapsulating why a client should choose your firm over competitors.

To craft a clear value proposition, you must first have a deep understanding of your target client's needs, challenges, and objectives. This insight, gained through the analysis process outlined earlier, will inform the specific benefits and value points that you should emphasize.

Your value proposition should address the following key elements:

- The client's pain points or challenges that you can solve
- The specific benefits or advantages that your company offers
- The unique value or differentiators that set you apart from competitors
- The tangible results or outcomes that the client can expect

For example, let's consider a value proposition for a cybersecurity consulting firm targeting small to medium-sized businesses:

"At CITADELA Consulting, we understand the unique cybersecurity challenges faced by growing businesses. Our team of certified ethical hackers and security experts will conduct a comprehensive risk assessment to identify vulnerabilities in your systems and infrastructure. Leveraging our proprietary security framework and state-of-the-art tools, we'll implement robust safeguards tailored to your specific needs, ensuring your critical data and networks are protected from emerging threats. With our proactive approach and continuous monitoring, you can have peace of mind knowing your business is secured against cyber-attacks, minimizing the risk of costly breaches and downtime."

In this example, the value proposition:

> Remember, your value proposition is the **cornerstone** of your Capability Statement, and it should be prominently featured and reinforced throughout the document. By crafting a **clear and compelling** value proposition, you can effectively communicate the unique value that your company can deliver to potential clients.

- Highlights the client's pain point (cybersecurity risks for growing businesses)
- Outlines the specific benefits (comprehensive risk assessment, tailored security solutions, continuous monitoring)
- Emphasizes the unique value (certified ethical hackers, proprietary security framework, state-of-the-art tools)
- Promises tangible results (protected from threats, minimized risk of breaches and downtime)

When crafting your value proposition, keep the following best practices in mind:

➤ Be concise and clear – aim for 2-3 sentences maximum
➤ Focus on the client's needs, not just your capabilities
➤ Use language and terminology that resonates with your target audience
➤ Quantify benefits and results where possible (e.g., "reduce costs by 25%")
➤ Highlight your key differentiators and what sets you apart

💡 In the space below, write a three-sentence paragraph describing your company's value. Use extra paper, if necessary.

(Intentionally left blank)

Compiling Case Studies and Relative Projects

A capability statement must include case studies since they are excellent instruments that demonstrate a business's knowledge, efficiency, and dependability. They provide a story that highlights a business's capacity for producing outcomes by fusing quantitative data with qualitative insights. Strategically including case studies into a capability statement can boost a business's credibility, show off its problem-solving skills, and give prospective customers a clear idea of what to expect. This explains the significance of case studies.

First and foremost, case studies offer verifiable proof of a business's accomplishments. By providing actual examples of completed projects, they go beyond simple declarations of capabilities. Prospective customers can observe the immediate results of the company's work thanks to this evidence-based strategy. A case study that demonstrates how a marketing firm raised a client's sales by 30% via a focused campaign, for example, offers compelling evidence of the agency's efficacy. Concrete proof of this kind has the potential to be far more convincing than generalized claims of competence.

Additionally, case studies provide thorough insights into a business's approaches and problem-solving abilities. Case studies illustrate a company's approach to and resolution of problems by detailing the difficulties encountered, the tactics used, and the results obtained. For prospective customers who wish to know how a business operates in addition to what it can accomplish, this openness is priceless. To demonstrate how it successfully performed a complex system integration for a client, for instance, an IT company may present a case study. This would include the technical difficulties, creative solutions found, and the project's successful conclusion. This degree of specificity contributes to increasing trust in the business's technical expertise and problem-solving skills.

Case studies help a corporation become more relatable while also showcasing its expertise. They convey a tale, frequently emphasizing the teamwork of the business and its beneficial effects on the client. A corporation can gain credibility and relatability by including this narrative aspect. When a business portrays itself as a partner dedicated to their success, rather than merely a service provider, prospective customers are more willing to interact with it. A consulting firm can demonstrate its dedication to client success by sharing a case study, for instance, of how it helped a small business turn around through strategic guidance. This kind of communication can connect with potential clients on a personal level.

Positive feedback is a gateway to compiling case studies for your proposals.

Case studies and relevant project examples are powerful tools for substantiating the claims made in your capability statement. They provide concrete evidence of your company's expertise, capabilities, and successful track record, helping to build credibility and trust with potential clients.

When compiling case studies and project examples, it's important to select those that are most relevant and impactful for your target audience. Consider the following factors:

- Industry or sector alignment: Choose projects that are within the same industry or sector as your target client. This demonstrates your familiarity and experience with their specific challenges and requirements.
- Project scope and complexity: Highlight projects that are similar in scope and complexity to the types of engagements

your target client is likely to require. This showcases your ability to handle projects of a comparable scale and level of difficulty.
- Achieved results and measurable outcomes: Prioritize case studies and projects where you can clearly demonstrate the tangible results and outcomes achieved. Quantifiable metrics, such as cost savings, increased efficiency, or improved performance, are particularly compelling.
- Client testimonials or feedback: Include direct quotes or testimonials from satisfied clients, as these provide third-party validation of your capabilities and the value you delivered.

When presenting case studies and project examples provide context by briefly describing the client's organization, industry, and the specific challenges or objectives they were facing.

In conclusion, case studies are a vital element of a capability statement. They provide concrete evidence of success, offer detailed insights into problem-solving methodologies, humanize the company, help potential clients envision positive outcomes, showcase versatility, and contribute to ongoing branding efforts. By effectively incorporating case studies, a company can significantly enhance its credibility and appeal to potential clients, ultimately supporting its business development efforts.

 What type of feedback loop exist within your company?

(Intentionally left blank)

Researching Metrics for Evaluations

In this segment we explore the indispensable role of metrics in crafting a compelling capability statement.

In this journey, we'll unravel the complexities of metrics, delving into their significance, types, methodologies, and ethical considerations.

Understanding metrics is not only crucial for evaluation research but also paramount for articulating your organization's strengths and capabilities

We discover why metrics are an essential component of a winning capability statement.

> When presenting case studies and project examples, provide context by *briefly describing* the client's organization, industry, and the *specific challenges* or objectives they were facing.

Before we get into the specifics, let's grasp the fundamental significance of metrics in capability statements. Metrics serve as tangible evidence of your organization's performance, impact, and effectiveness in delivering products or services. They provide quantifiable measures of success, validating your claims and distinguishing your organization from competitors. Incorporating relevant metrics in your capability statement not only enhances credibility but also instills confidence in potential clients, partners, or funders. By demonstrating your track record of success through metrics, you can showcase your organization's capacity to deliver results and fulfill stakeholders' needs.

Metrics encompass a diverse array of measures, each serving a unique purpose in conveying your organization's capabilities. From financial performance indicators to customer satisfaction metrics, the types of metrics you include in your capability statement depend on your industry, target audience, and strategic objectives. Financial metrics such as revenue growth, profit margins, or return on investment demonstrate your organization's financial health and stability.

Operational metrics such as productivity rates, turnaround times, or error rates showcase your efficiency and effectiveness in delivering services or products.

Customer satisfaction metrics such as Net Promoter Score (NPS) or customer retention rates highlight your commitment to meeting client needs and fostering long-term relationships.

As stewards of data integrity and ethical conduct, it's essential to consider ethical considerations when researching and presenting metrics in your capability statement.

Respect for privacy, confidentiality, and informed consent is paramount when collecting data from individuals or organizations. Researchers must adhere to ethical guidelines and regulatory requirements governing data collection, storage, and usage to protect stakeholders' rights and mitigate risks of harm or misuse.

By adopting a systematic approach to researching metrics, you can gather robust evidence to support your organization's claims and differentiate your capability statement from competitors.

> *By adopting a systematic approach to researching metrics, you can gather robust evidence to support your organization's claims and differentiate your capability statement from competitors.*

By strategically selecting and presenting these metrics in your capability statement, you can paint a comprehensive picture of your organization's strengths, capabilities, and value proposition. Whether you're vying for government contracts, seeking partnerships, or attracting investors, metrics serve as powerful Evidence of your organization's ability to deliver results and drive success.

Crafting a winning capability statement requires rigorous research and analysis to Identify, collect, and interpret relevant metrics. Researchers must employ sound methodologies and data collection techniques to ensure the validity, reliability, and relevance of the metrics presented. Qualitative research methods such as interviews, focus groups, or case studies can provide rich insights into customer experiences, organizational culture, or market dynamics.

Quantitative research methods such as surveys, financial analysis, or performance metrics offer numerical data to quantify outcomes, assess performance, and track progress over time.

As stewards of data integrity and ethical conduct, it's essential to consider ethical considerations when researching and presenting metrics in your capability statement.

Respect for privacy, confidentiality, and informed consent is paramount when collecting data from individuals or organizations. Researchers must adhere to ethical guidelines and regulatory requirements governing data collection, storage, and usage to protect stakeholders' rights and mitigate risks of harm or misuse.

Furthermore, transparency and accountability are essential when presenting metrics in your capability statement. Clearly communicate the sources, methodologies, and limitations of the metrics presented, acknowledging any biases or uncertainties that may affect their interpretation. By upholding ethical principles and promoting transparency, you can build trust and credibility with your audience, strengthening your organization's reputation and integrity.

When researching metrics for your capability statement, consider the following questions ~

Do I have key performance indicators?

Key performance indicators (KPIs) are important to measure within a company so that any client or competitor can know your rate of success.

What data sources are available to collect relevant metrics?

Not all data is created equal. Decide what data sources are available for your specific needs.

Can you ensure the accuracy and reliability of the metrics presented?

Nothing speaks to incompetency like presenting bad or defunct data. Ensure that your source is reliable and have a method of verifying.

Are the metrics aligned with your company's area of expertise?

Don't make the mistake of presenting general data for presentation. Your client's needs are specific to them, and you want to ensure you have data that reflects this.

As we conclude our exploration of metrics in crafting a winning capability statement, remember the transformative power of data-driven storytelling and evidence-based communication. By incorporating relevant metrics, employing sound methodologies, and upholding ethical standards, you can elevate your capability statement from a mere document to a persuasive tool for showcasing your organization's strengths and capabilities. Whether you're competing for contracts, seeking partnerships, or attracting investors, let metrics be your guiding star in demonstrating your organization's capacity to deliver value and drive success.

As you embark on your journey to craft a winning capability statement, may the insights gained from this segment empower you to navigate the complexities of metrics with confidence and purpose.

 What are your primary KPIs?

(Intentionally left blank)

Effectively Summarizing Your Core Competencies

A compelling capability statement will resonate with stakeholders, differentiates your organization from competitors, and opens doors to new opportunities for collaboration and growth.

In this segment, we'll explore the significance of core competencies, their role in crafting a compelling capability statement, and the acceptable formats for presenting them. Whether you're a small business owner, a seasoned entrepreneur, or a government contractor, mastering core competencies is essential for showcasing your organization's strengths and capabilities. Join us as we dive into the world of core competencies and learn how to create an impactful capability statement that sets you apart from the competition.

Core competencies represent the unique strengths, skills, and capabilities that distinguish an organization from its competitors. They encompass the collective knowledge, expertise, and resources that enable an organization to deliver value to its clients, customers, or stakeholders. By identifying and leveraging core competencies, organizations can gain a competitive advantage, drive innovation, and achieve sustainable growth in dynamic markets.

In the context of capability statements, core competencies serve as the foundation for articulating your organization's value proposition, differentiating yourself from competitors, and attracting potential clients, partners, or investors. They provide a snapshot of your organization's key strengths, capabilities, and areas of expertise, enabling stakeholders to quickly assess your suitability for collaboration or partnership opportunities.

When summarizing core competencies for a capability statement, it's essential to consider the following key components:

1. **Technical Expertise**: Highlight your organization's technical skills, knowledge, and qualifications relevant to your industry or sector. This may include certifications, licenses, specialized training, or industry-specific expertise that demonstrate your proficiency in delivering products or services.

2. **Experience and Track Record**: Showcase your organization's track record of success, including past performance, case studies, client testimonials, or awards and recognitions.

Providing concrete examples of your accomplishment's outcomes can enhance credibility and instill confidence in new potential clients or partners.

3. **Differentiators and Unique Value Proposition (UVP)**: Identify the unique aspects of your organization that set you apart from competitors. This may include proprietary technologies, innovative approaches, strategic partnerships, or a niche market focus that differentiate your organization and create value for stakeholders.

4. **Resources and Capabilities**: Outline the resources, infrastructure, and capabilities that support your organization's operations and service delivery. This may include physical assets, intellectual property, human capital, or strategic alliances that contribute to your organization's ability to meet client needs and deliver results.

Acceptable Formats for Presenting Core Competencies

Structured Narrative

Present core competencies in a concise, narrative format that highlights key strengths, achievements, and capabilities. Organize information logically, using bullet points or short paragraphs to convey key messages and examples of relevant experience.

Bullet Point Format

Utilize bullet points to list core competencies in a clear, concise manner. This format allows for easy scanning and comprehension, making it ideal for quickly conveying key information to busy stakeholders.

Visual Infographics

Create visually appealing infographics or charts to illustrate core competencies and key performance indicators. Visual representations can enhance engagement, comprehension, and retention of information, particularly for complex or technical content.

Tabular Format

Organize core competencies in a tabular format, with columns for different categories such as technical expertise, experience, dIfferentiators, and resources. This format provides a structured framework for presenting information and allows stakeholders to compare and contrast key attributes easily.

 **REMEMBER...**

Avoid overwhelming stakeholders with excessive detail or technical jargon, and ensure that the core competencies highlighted align closely with the requirements of potential clients, partners, or funding agencies.

Let your core competencies be the cornerstone of your capability statement, guiding stakeholders towards a deeper understanding of your organization's value proposition and potential for success.

Resources

SMART2GO Training® - smart2gotraining.com
Providing specialized knowledge in the area of real estate investing, leadership training, and personal/professional development.

Capability Statement Templates – smart2gotraining.com/shop

Capability Statement FREE Course - smart2gotraining.com/course/craft-a-compelling-capability-statement

Note: All digital products sold on the smart2gotraining.com website is Non-Refundable, including courses and printable templates.

Email – admin@smart2gotraining.com

(Intentionally left blank)

www.ingramcontent.com/pod-product-compliance
Lightning Source LLC
Chambersburg PA
CBHW072005210526
45479CB00003B/1079